MASTERBUILDERS

This book belongs to:

....

Age:

....

A LEGO Media Book

First published in the United States in 2000 by LEGO Systems, Inc.
555 Taylor Road, P.O. Box 1600, Enfield, CT 06083-1600

Reprinted in 2000

10 9 8 7 6 5 4 3 2

Join the LEGO Community
www.LEGO.com

ISBN 1903 276160

Colour reproduction by Anglia Graphics
Manufactured in China by Leo Paper Products Ltd.

Check out other cool toys in the LEGO Space Port range:

MARS MISSION
MASTERBUILDERS

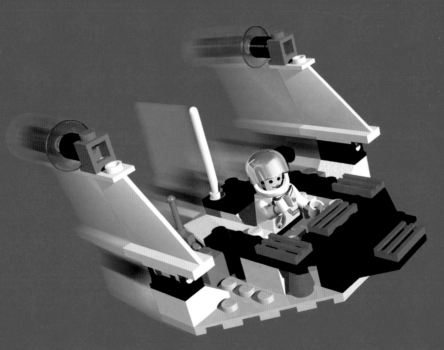

Illustrator **Sebastian Quigley**

Managing Editor **Anne Marie Ryan**

Senior Designer **Stephen Scanlan**

Contents

Number of models = 15

6 Introduction

Do you want to become a LEGO Masterbuilder? **Mars Mission** will show you how. Specially developed with the help of professional LEGO model-makers, this book lets young apprentices like you learn from the experts. Work your way through the fun models featured in **Mars Mission** and you will be a Masterbuilder in no time at all!

The models in this book range in difficulty from easy, to medium and difficult. Try warming up with the simple models before tackling the more challenging vehicles. Special symbols on each page will show you the level of difficulty and how many bricks are used in the model, not counting the Mini figure.

All the LEGO bricks you need to make each model in this book are included in the plastic box. Before you start building a model, it is helpful to find all the LEGO bricks that you will use and put them to one side. Store the bricks back in the plastic box when you have finished building so they don't get lost.

After you have built a model, you can decorate it however you like. The plastic box includes a sheet of stickers, which you can use to customize your spacecraft. Add these cool symbols and logos to your shuttles and satellites!

There are 15 amazing models to make in this book, but that is just the beginning. There is no limit to the amazing creations you can construct with your LEGO bricks! Just let your imagination run free and you will think of hundreds of LEGO models to build.

Part of the fun of making LEGO models is taking them apart and building something new. Once you have had fun playing with a model, you can turn it into something else! Keep track of which models you have built by filling out the chart at the back of the book. When your certificate is complete, you will be an official LEGO Masterbuilder!

How to use this book:

Follow the numbered steps to build your models.

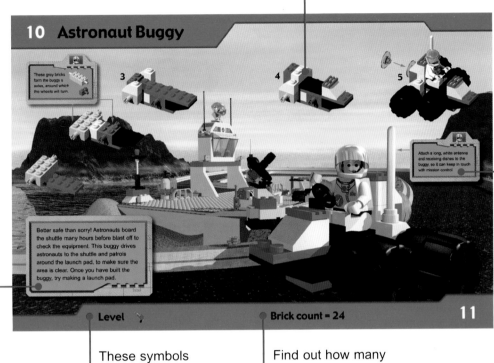

10 Astronaut Buggy

These grey bricks form the buggy's axles, around which the wheels will turn.

3

4

5

Attach a long, white antenna and receiving dishes to the buggy, so it can keep in touch with mission control

Better safe than sorry! Astronauts board the shuttle many hours before blast off to check the equipment. This buggy drives astronauts to the shuttle and patrols around the launch pad, to make sure the area is clear. Once you have built the buggy, try making a launch pad.

Level

Brick count = 24

11

These boxes will help you with some of the trickier steps.

This box gives you great ideas for playing with your finished model.

These symbols show you the level of difficulty.

Find out how many LEGO bricks are used in the model.

Making your Mini figure:

Before you start building models, here is how to put together your LEGO Mini figure. This guy is a veteran astronaut who cannot wait to be the first man on Mars!

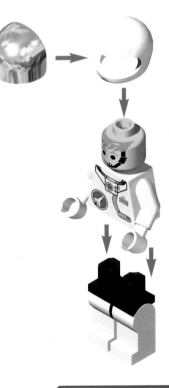

Give your astronaut a sporty cap for ground control duties.

Your astronaut wears a helmet for survival in deep space.

Blast Off!

5… 4… 3… 2… 1… Blast off! The ground crew prepares the shuttle and astronauts for the launch. After countdown, the shuttle's engines ignite and its rockets propel the craft deep into space. Launch your imagination and start building these out-of-this-world models!

Shuttle Transporter
This load weighs a ton! A strong truck wheels the heavy shuttle to the launch pad. *Page 16.*

Mission Control
Earth, do you read me? A team of experts monitors the shuttle at mission control. *Page 12.*

Astronaut Buggy
All aboard! This fast little buggy takes the astronauts to the waiting shuttle. *Page 10.*

Space Shuttle
Up, up and away! The space shuttle prepares to blast off on its mission to Mars.
Page 18.

Repair Center
Waste not, want not! The repair center mends old spacecraft so they can be reused. *Page 14.*

Number of models = 5

Astronaut Buggy

These grey bricks form the buggy's axles, around which the wheels will turn.

3

2

1

Better safe than sorry! Astronauts board the shuttle many hours before blast off to check the equipment. This buggy drives astronauts to the shuttle and patrols around the launch pad to make sure the area is clear. Once you have built the buggy, try making a launch pad.

Level

4

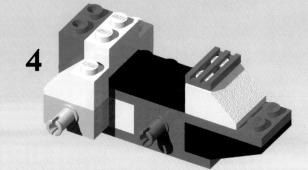

5

Attach a long white antenna and receiving dishes to the buggy so it can keep in touch with mission control.

Brick count = 24

Mission Control

1

2

3

This radio dish is on a hinge so it can move to catch signals from all directions, including distant planets!

 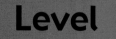

1

2

3

Don't forget to add a walkie-talkie, so the mission control crew can stay in touch even when they are on the go.

Houston, we have a problem…
At mission control, big computer screens track the shuttle. Giant radio dishes pick up satellite signals from the craft so the ground crew can talk to the astronauts. Can you guide your astronaut through an emergency landing?

Brick count = 26

14 Repair Center

New shuttles are very expensive to make. At this repair center, mechanics carefully mend all sorts of spacecraft – from little buggies to big shuttles – to make them as good as new. Build up these two vehicles then send them on an exciting mission!

1

Build some red thrusters on to the back of the shuttle, to give it the power to launch into space.

2

3

1

2

3

When you add wheels and a clear blue windscreen to this buggy it will be ready to roll once more!

4

4

Brick count = 43

Shuttle Transporter

A space shuttle can travel deep into space, but first it must get to the launch pad! This special, heavy-duty transporter wheels the shuttle across the space center. When you have built the transporter, turn to the next page to find out how to build a shuttle.

1

Useful tools, such as a hammer and a walkie-talkie, attach to the grey hooks at the back.

2

3

Level

It is difficult to see it in this picture, but be sure to add a steering wheel to the transporter.

Brick count = 39

18 Space Shuttle

1

To make the satellite's base, place a sloped white brick on either side of the long white brick, but do not connect them.

2

3

Level

1

2

3

Ladies and gentlemen, we have lift off! This shuttle will carry the astronauts to Mars. When you have built the shuttle, you can also make a satellite dish to track its progress. Try wheeling your shuttle around on the transporter, or practice blasting off from a launch pad.

Brick count = 30

METSAT

Looks like rain down there! A METSAT can predict weather weeks, even decades, in advance. *Page 26.*

Space Station

Check out the view! A space station is in orbit for a very long time, as its crew studies life in space. *Page 28.*

Once the shuttle reaches deep space it goes into orbit. This means that it travels around a planet. In orbit, a shuttle opens its cargo doors and releases satellites. Satellites have many different uses, from weather forecasting to communications, and even spying!

COMSAT

Ring, ring! Is anyone there? A COMSAT relays telephone and television signals around the world. *Page 22.*

Orbiter

Stop, I'm feeling dizzy! The orbiter is the part of a shuttle that travels round and round a planet. *Page 24.*

Number of models = 4

COMSAT

When you watch television or make a telephone call, you are being helped by COMSATs, or communications satellites. COMSATs receive signals from Earth and bounce them back to a different location. Can you build a tower to receive signals from your COMSAT?

1

2

The black disc can spin around, which allows the satellite to pick up signals from all directions.

3

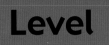 **Level**

Remember to add the receiving dish, so the satellite can get signals from Earth and send them back.

4

5

Brick count = 28

Being in orbit is no pleasure cruise! An orbiter has many jobs to do as it circles a planet. It might release new satellites or repair old ones. The orbiter may also dock with a space station to deliver a fresh crew or supplies. Why not build a satellite for your orbiter to release?

1

The grey wings and blue bricks should be placed next to each other, but do not join them together right now.

2

5

4

The blue brick at the back of the orbiter has a hole in its middle, through which the tail lights can attach.

3

Brick count = 53

1

2

3

Level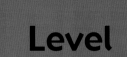

How do weathermen know when it will rain? Meteorological Satellites, or METSATs, help to predict the weather. METSATs send pictures of cloud patterns to Earth. If your satellite needs repairs, build a space pack for the astronaut to wear while fixing it.

4

5

Attach a handy hammer and walkie-talkie to the satellite, in case any repairs need to be made in space.

6

Brick count = 16

1

2

3

To make the base of the space station, position the blue brick next to the grey brick, but do not connect them yet.

Level

Would you like to live in space? Then a space station is the place for you! The crew of a space station lives on board and conducts scientific experiments about life in space. Try building the inside of a space station. Can you send your astronaut on a space walk?

4

5

Give your space station some bright red lights so that docking spacecraft will be able to see it!

6

Get ready to make history as your astronaut becomes the first human on Mars. During touchdown, the landing craft separates from the orbiter. Mars is covered with craters, some as deep as the Grand Canyon. So, fasten your seat belt and prepare for a bumpy landing!

Hover Scout

Do you see any place to park? The hover scout searches the planet's surface for a smooth landing spot. *Page 32.*

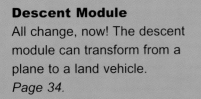

Descent Module
All change, now! The descent module can transform from a plane to a land vehicle.
Page 34.

Number of models = 2

Hover Scout

The hover scout is specially designed for cruising just above a planet's surface. It uses powerful radar to search for good landing spots on Mars. You can move the scout's wings up and down as it zooms around looking for smooth surfaces without any craters.

This sloped brick is the control panel. It has computer systems that help the astronaut to navigate.

1

2

Level

5

4

3

Remember to add the hinges, as they will allow you to raise and lower the wings on your hover scout.

Brick count = 47

Descent Module

One small step for man, one giant leap for mankind! Your astronaut will be the first person to explore Mars in this descent module. This multi-purpose vehicle has removable wings. When your astronaut lands, you can replace the wings with four wheels.

1

2

Level

Be sure to have a walkie-talkie on board, because your astronaut may need to contact the mother ship!

6

5

3

4

Brick count = 52

Drilling Robot

What's the drill? This robot cuts through the planet's surface collecting rock samples. *Page 42.*

Is there anybody out there? Your astronaut is on a mission to find out whether there is life on Mars. Deep craters and volcanoes make it hard to travel on the Red Planet. You can help the astronaut by building robots and vehicles for exloring Mars.

Rock Rover
Hang on tight, this will be a bumpy ride! Your astronaut can explore the planet's rocky surface in a sturdy rover. *Page 40.*

Planet Probe
Say cheese! A probe photographs the surface of a planet, looking for signs of life. *Page 44.*

Astro Lab
Eureka! Your astronaut can carry out important scientific experiments in the astro lab. *Page 38.*

Number of models = 4

38 Astro Lab

The crew builds an astro lab on the surface of Mars. They use the lab to measure temperatures and analyze rock samples. Scientists will study whether there is fuel or water on Mars, and if humans could ever survive there. What would a house on Mars look like? Try building one!

1

2

Level

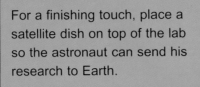

For a finishing touch, place a satellite dish on top of the lab so the astronaut can send his research to Earth.

6

5

3

4

40 Rock Rover

Astronauts can explore the bumpy surface of Mars quickly in this tough, jeep-like vehicle. The rock rover has special wheels to scramble over the planet's rocks and climb up steep hills. Why not test how your rover handles on rocky ground?

1

Level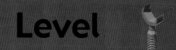

2

3

Don't forget to add the control panel so the astronaut can track his journey across the planet.

4

5

Brick count = 41

42 Drilling Robot

1

2

3

Level

4

This remote-controlled robot roams over the surface of Mars. It drills deep down under the planet's surface to collect soil samples. Scientists will study the rocks, looking for fossils and evidence of life on Mars. Can you make some strange fossils for your robot to find?

5

At the front of the robot, add two red lights that can send out laser beams powerful enough to cut through rock!

6

7

1

2

The planet probe takes photographs of Mars and transmits the images back to mission control. So far, no probes on Mars have found signs of life. But this powerful probe might just be the first. What do you imagine Martians to look like? Try building a model of a Martian.

3

4

Don't forget to add on a steering wheel so that your astronaut can drive the probe around Mars.

5

Level

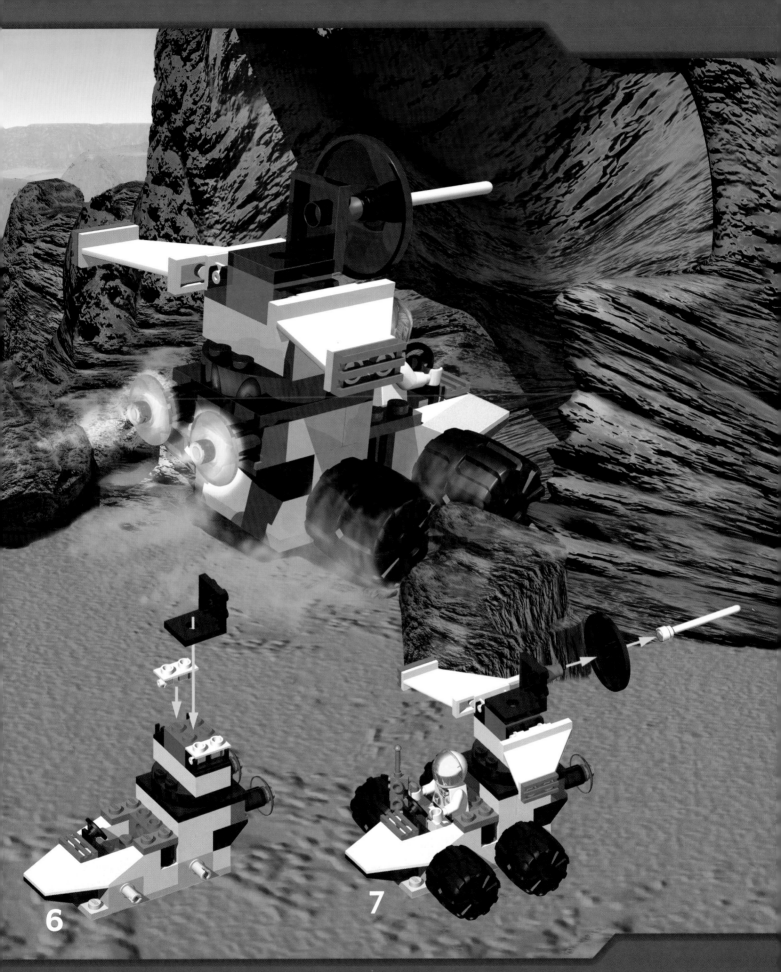

Certificate

When you complete a model, fill in the date and how much time it took you to build it on this chart. If you make every model in the book, you will become a LEGO Masterbuilder!

Astronaut Buggy

Date built: _____   Time spent: _____

Mission Control

Date built: _____   Time spent: _____

Repair Center

Date built: _____   Time spent: _____

Shuttle Transporter

Date built: _____   Time spent: _____

Space Shuttle

Date built: _____   Time spent: _____

COMSAT

Date built: _____   Time spent: _____

Orbiter

Date built: _____   Time spent: _____

METSAT

Date built: _____ Time spent: _____

Space Station

Date built: _____ Time spent: _____

Hover Scout

Date built: _____ Time spent: _____

Descent Module

Date built: _____ Time spent: _____

Astro Lab

Date built: _____ Time spent: _____

Rock Rover

Date built: _____ Time spent: _____

Drilling Robot

Date built: _____ Time spent: _____

Planet Probe

Date built: _____ Time spent: _____

Congratulations! You are now officially a LEGO Masterbuilder.